CLASSIFIED

You can't hide the truth forever

D1031242

Vanished!

TERRY DEARY

KINGFISHER

KINGFISHER
An imprint of Kingfisher Publications Plc
New Penderel House, 283–288 High Holborn
London WC1V 7HZ
www.kingfisherpub.com

First published by Kingfisher 1996
This edition published by Kingfisher 2004

2 4 6 8 10 9 7 5 3 1

Text copyright © Terry Deary 1996

A CIP catalogue record for this book
is available from the British Library.

ISBN 0 7534 1021 4

Printed in India
1TR/0504/THOM/MA/115IWF

CONTENTS PAGE

INTRODUCTION

The universe is not only stranger than we imagine. It is stranger than we *can* imagine. It has its mysteries – and it has its secrets.

But mysteries and secrets are not necessarily the same thing.

There are many puzzles about the universe that are not secrets at all. How did the universe begin? When was it born? What existed before that? Nobody knows the answers to these puzzles. They are mysteries. People come up with ideas, scientists look for ways to prove them and slowly the mysteries are solved.

But there are some puzzles to which someone, somewhere does know the answer. Answers that they choose to hide from the rest of the world. Secrets.

Some secrets are so frightening that governments think we will panic if they are ever exposed. Has the Earth been visited by alien life forms? Are there weapons so powerful that they are capable of destroying every living thing on Earth? Have scientists conducted experiments so disastrous that they are ashamed to tell us what they did?

Secrets like these are so potentially explosive that the authorities try to cover them up. They create a whole new world of lies to show that the thing never happened. And they set about destroying every last scrap of evidence. What if that evidence is in the memory of some human witness? Can they destroy that witness? The answer is yes. Many governments in history have kept secrets by murdering the witnesses.

It seems incredible that with all these efforts to cover up the truth, stories do sometimes leak out. Stories like that of a warship that became invisible! The government says it never happened, but still the stories persist. So many stories that you simply have to ask yourself could it really have happened? Could a warship disappear into thin air? Is there any truth in this incredible story – the story of the Philadelphia Experiment?

The truth must exist somewhere. But the evidence has remained deliberately hidden. It has been locked away in files that only a few people are ever allowed to read. Files marked:

CLASSIFIED

CHAPTER ONE

I always knew that one day I'd be caught. I didn't know when they'd come for me, I didn't know who they'd send and I didn't quite picture how they'd do it.

They came at four in the morning, when a loud knocking at the door dragged me from an exhausted sleep. I reached for a dressing gown but didn't bother with slippers as I padded along the cold wooden floor of the hallway. The chain was on the door so it opened just a few centimetres. "What do you want?" I asked.

"Miss Henreid?" someone asked from the shadows of the porch. It was a woman's voice. I hadn't expected that. Deep and husky as if she smoked too many cigarettes, but a woman's voice. I should have known the way their minds' worked. They'd sent a woman to make the situation seem less threatening.

"Who are you?" I asked and groped for the switch by the door. The porch light snapped on and I squinted through the crack in the doorway and saw them. There were two of them. He was exactly what I expected – a man in a dark suit, with neat hair and a blank expression on a forgettable face. She wore a charcoal grey suit with a faint chalk stripe, dark stockings and a plain cream blouse. Her ash-grey hair was cut short and styled expensively to frame her face, but it did nothing to soften her cold, grey eyes. I'm no expert on female beauty but I guess she would have been pretty if it hadn't been for her jawline being a little too strong and her lips a little too thin.

The man had an identity card ready and held it up so I could see his picture. The light wasn't good enough for me to read the details. "FBI?" I asked.

"DIA," she said, holding up her card too.

"CIA? Central Intelligence Agency?" I checked.

"No," he said quietly. "DIA. Defense Intelligence Agency."

I hadn't known about them and I suppose my doubt showed in my face. The woman seemed a little impatient as she said, "We're from the Office of Naval Intelligence within the DIA."

That made sense. Naval Intelligence. They were the people I'd been trying to steal secrets from. Now they'd caught me. I felt my shoulders sag in defeat. "May we come in?" the man asked softly. His blank face seemed to have a little more warmth in it now. Sighing, I unfastened the chain and held the door open.

"Can I get dressed?" I asked. The two agents glanced at one another.

"I'll come with you," the woman said.

I hesitated for a moment. I knew I wouldn't feel comfortable dressing in front of her. "It's alright, I'm not going to try to escape!" I joked.

Her thin mouth narrowed even more, and turned down at the corners. "We just want to ask you a few questions. We're not planning to put you in front of a firing squad."

I wasn't reassured. "So why watch me while I dress?"

"Standard procedure," the man explained and he raised one shoulder slightly in a shrug of apology.

"There is always the possibility that you may conceal or destroy evidence while you are alone in your room," the woman said. Her voice was harsh.

I knew that all the evidence against me was hidden in files in my computer. Entry was barred by codes and passwords that would require a genius to crack. In my opinion all relevant information was locked away as securely as if it had been in a safe bolted to the wall of the Titanic. More securely, in fact.

I walked back along the hallway to my room. At least she had the decency to pretend to inspect my computer as I pulled my pyjamas off and dressed quickly in a track suit and trainers. I ran a comb through my shoulder length hair and frightened myself by looking in the mirror over my dressing table. No one looks their best at 4 am and I was no exception. My green eyes, usually clear and sparkling, were surrounded by dark shadows and my mouth was framed by tiny lines which gave away how tired and tense I felt.

"I'll have to let my grandfather know where I'm going," I said.

The woman turned slowly, narrowed her eyes and looked at me. "I don't think there's any need to worry the old gentleman," she said. "If you answer our questions then you should be home before he wakes up."

"He doesn't know anything about this." I was lying, but it was a white lie. "I wouldn't want him to be upset."

She gave a soft snort through her wide, dark nostrils. "You should have thought of the worry you'd be causing him when you began breaking the law," she said. Then she gave a nod of her head to show that I should leave the room. I picked up a notepad and pen that were lying on my bedside table and scribbled a quick note to my grandfather, just in case I didn't come back. I intended to push it under the door to his room, but when I got there, I hesitated. If he woke before I returned then he'd guess I'd simply gone out early. That wasn't so unusual. I screwed up the note and pushed it into my pocket.

The man was waiting in the hallway. He seemed to look right through me as I locked the door and then they both escorted me to a dark Chevy, placed me in the back of the car and drove silently to the centre of town.

The sun was lightening the slate sky with lemon ribbons of light as we swung into an underground car park beneath a large grey building. It occurred to me that I might never see the sunrise again. I know that sounds dramatic, but I was seriously scared that they'd lock me up and throw away the key. That's the trouble with a guilty conscience. You imagine they know everything about you. When you think about it, they can't. After all, they wouldn't be taking me in for questioning if they already knew everything.

We rode up in a lift to the tenth floor and stepped out into a quiet, air-conditioned corridor with about a dozen doors leading off it. It seemed more like an hotel than a government building.

The man opened a door and held it open while I walked into a small office. It was nothing like I'd imagined. I'd expected a steel chair, handcuffs and a desk-lamp shining on my face as they repeated question after question. Instead, there was a desk with a leather swivel chair and three comfortable chairs around a coffee table. There were no clues to give away what sort of business went on behind these walls. It seemed as if it was going to be more like a cosy interview for a job in a petrol station. Maybe that was their plan. Get me to relax so they could catch me off guard. It wasn't going to work. I was very scared and that made me twice as wary.

"Expecting the rubber truncheons?" the woman said and gave me a smile as sweet as vinegar.

I think my mouth fell open at the thought that she was reading my mind. "No," I managed to say. "I've done nothing wrong."

"Of course not," she breathed, with a hint of sarcasm. "Let's start, shall we?"

"Sure," I said. I tried to make myself relax into the chair as the agents picked up clip-boards with sheets of paper attached.

"Your name?"

"You know it," I said.

The woman tightened her grip on her pen but said nothing. After a moment the man leaned forward and spoke softly. "We're at the early stages of an investigation. This is not a formal interview, just a chat. But we do have to go through certain procedures just the same. We have to make sure that you are the person we want to interview. That's all." He sounded so reasonable that he made me feel like a delinquent child in class. Still I stalled.

"I don't believe I caught your names," I said.

He nodded. "I'm Agent Miller, and this is Agent Kirwan," he said, inclining his head towards the woman. "And you are?"

"Alice Henreid," I answered automatically – then bit my tongue. He was smooth, I had to hand it to him. I knew then and there that he was going to get my story out of me whereas she never would.

"Tell us a little about yourself, Alice," he said and sat back. The expression on his face seemed to indicate that he was genuinely interested. Up until this moment in my life, and including it I guess, I had led a rather lonely existence. I had always been an outsider. Hardly anyone had ever shown much interest in me in the past – except my grandfather, of course. And now here I was, the centre of attention, being asked to sit and talk about myself. I felt almost flattered. Maybe, I thought, I could just tell them a little. And so I started to talk.

CHAPTER TWO

"I'm a mathematician," I began.

Agent Miller nodded but prompted, "No. Go back a little way. Tell us how you came to be where you are today. When did you first get interested in maths? How come you're living with your grandfather, Professor Henreid?"

"My mother was a mathematician. I guess she picked it up from her father – the grandfather I live with. He's nuts about maths and she was very bright as a kid. Graduated and had a great career ahead of her." I sighed, indicating that things had not exactly gone according to plan in her life.

"What went wrong?" he asked perceptively.

"Who really knows? Her version of what happened is that at that time it was impossible for a woman to succeed in the maths world. She said men never took her seriously. In discussions they acted like she wasn't even there. She'd make a suggestion and her male colleagues would ignore her. Then, 20 minutes later, one of them would repeat her idea and the others would enthuse about it. But maybe she just wasn't strong enough or determined enough to succeed."

Agent Kirwan gave that soft snort through her nose and muttered, "That still happens, *especially* in government agencies."

"Well, it drove her crazy. In the end she dropped out of the college circuit – 'the circus' as she called it – and married a mechanic."

"Then you were born?" Agent Miller asked.

"Sure. But my parents weren't really interested in me. They were young and I tied them down. When I was about three or four years old, my grandfather came to visit. He noticed something about the way I was playing and reckoned that I was a smart kid and that I possibly had a good mathematical brain. He offered to take me away and educate me himself. Basically he wanted to get me away from my – shall we say – 'free spirited' parents. They didn't exactly fight hard to hang onto me," I finished. I knew I must have sounded bitter, but I didn't really care.

As it turned out, Grandfather was the best thing that ever happened to me. Some kids have grandfathers who show them how to ride a bike or tell them stories about the 'good old days'. *My* grandfather showed me how to solve complicated maths problems and told me stories about all kinds of science experiments he'd been involved in. Experiments so weird that when he told people about them, they didn't believe him. In the end he gave up talking about the experiments to anyone but me. He opened my young mind up to a whole new world.

And I believed everything he told me. Not because he was my grandfather and not because I was just a child who didn't know any better. I believed him because I had a mathematical brain and it all made sense. Gradually, as I grew up, I began to totally immerse myself in the world of mathematics and physics.

I guess that's where the story of the Philadelphia Experiment fits in. Certainly how it all began for me. You see, one of the stories Grandfather told me was about a warship that disappeared. I don't mean sank or went missing after a storm – it literally vanished into thin air, then reappeared just as suddenly.

I don't remember when he first told me that story but I reckon I must have been about 13 years old at the time. He told me that it was all part of an important experiment. He explained his role in the experiment to me. By the time I was 14 I knew it backwards and started my own calculations to check it out for myself.

After that I put it aside for a while. Then some time later – I suppose about a couple of years later – I remember coming

7

home from school one evening and asking Grandfather to run through some calculations with me. I had to do a project for school and I had decided to work on an advanced mathematical theory.

He looked up from his desk and asked me. "What are you up to then, Alice?"

"The Philadelphia Experiment and Einstein's Unified Field Theory," I replied. "I intend to prove two things. First, that the Experiment happened, and second, that Einstein's Unified Field Theory is more than just a theory."

Grandfather ran a hand over the white hair that sat on his head like a cockatoo's crest. His faded blue eyes sparkled as he looked at me over the top of his half-moon glasses, but he wasn't laughing. "Most people believe that Einstein never finished the Unified Field Theory," he said.

"But you believe he *did* finish it, don't you, Grandfather?" I said. "Tell me the story again about how you met him back in 1943." I wanted to encourage him to be part of my plan.

He pushed himself stiffly to his feet. He straightened from the waist but his shoulders remained rounded from too many hours spent poring over calculations at his ancient oak desk. We strolled out to the back porch and looked over the rough grass towards the sinking orange ball of the Sun. As it began to dip below the treetops, he told me again the story of the Philadelphia Experiment. But this time he told me more – much more.

"It was during World War II. I was a very junior scientist working for the Naval Defence Research Committee," he began.

"Making secret weapons?" I asked.

He frowned. "More than that. We were trying to come up with completely new ideas to win the War. Let me give you an example. Say you want to kill your enemy. The obvious thing is to punch a hole in them till they bleed to death. Cave men did it with spears and arrows, we do it with bullets, but the basic idea is the same. Spears or bullets are the same *type* of weapon – they have the same effect. Now in World War I the enemies began using poison gas. That doesn't make your enemy bleed to death, it makes them suffocate. It's a new kind of weapon. Then in the Second World War we tried bombing women and children in the big cities – this time the weapon was terror. Again, you see, a new kind of weapon. And radar was a new weapon too – just being able to see your enemy when he was still 80 kilometres away. Submarines sinking warships wasn't a new weapon, but submarines sinking food supply ships to starve the British, that *was* a new weapon! Get the idea?"

"I understand," I nodded. "Parachutes were really a new weapon too, because they meant you could move soldiers behind enemy lines and attack them from behind."

My grandfather smiled.

"Exactly. You wouldn't believe some of the secret weapons that were dreamed up in the Second World War. One scientist came up with the idea of spraying frozen sawdust over enemy shipyards so the ports would be paralysed!"

"What has all this got to do with Albert Einstein?" I asked.

"Einstein was born in Germany but he hated Adolf Hitler and the Nazi Party. He hated their nationalism. He said nationalism was an infant sickness... the measles of the human race. A great man, Einstein," Grandfather said and his eyes glistened as he recalled his colleague.

"So he came to America?"

"He came to *help* America. You understand he was a mathematician, not a weapon maker. Albert Einstein came up with theories – our job was to make them work in practice."

"That's when you met him?"

"Certainly. But don't forget, I was still just a young man. I wasn't in on the very top secret plans. They used me rather the way you use a pocket calculator. Like a pocket calculator, I came up with the right answers, but I didn't know why they were needed. All I could do was guess. Remember, I knew

9

about Einstein's Unified Field Theory, I knew the scientists he came to meet and I put two and two together. I reckoned they were planning to create the perfect defensive weapon. You remember the Star Ship Enterprise on Star Trek?"

I nodded. "It defends itself with an invisible shield." I said. "Some kind of force field."

"Exactly! Imagine sending your tanks, your warships and your airplanes into battle protected by that invisible shield! You could go forward into the very heart of the enemy and destroy without being destroyed. The War would be over in a week!"

"But no one has invented that invisible shield. It's just science fiction," I argued. "Just something you see on Star Trek."

Grandfather looked at me carefully and spoke slowly. "Don't be so sure, Alice," he smiled gently. "Don't be so sure."

CHAPTER THREE

Grandfather always gave me good advice. He explained what I'd have to do if I wanted to get my project off to a good start. "You have to remember, Alice, your teachers aren't as advanced as you are when it comes to maths. When you present your work you'll need to explain the theory the way you would to a child. Begin by explaining Einstein's Unified Field Theory."

"Fine. Where do I start?" I said without hesitating, glad that Grandfather was willing to be involved.

"You know how to make electricity?" he asked.

I knew how to make electricity alright. When other kids were pushing toy cars around the floor of the school I was building trucks that ran on electric motors. I think Grandfather gave me the electrical assembly kit for my sixth birthday. Within a week I'd mastered it.

I know the other kids at school thought I was a little weird, but they liked the gadgets I made. It was some of the teachers I had trouble with! One day, a certain teacher – Miss Markham – asked, "Wouldn't you be happier playing with the dolls in the play house, Alice?" I guess that was the first time I ever used the withering, 'Are you talking to *me?*' look that I was to perfect over the years. She and I were never on good terms after that.

So I knew about electricity. "Turn a magnet in a coil of wire and you create electricity in the wire," I said.

"Or?"

"Or put electricity through the coil of wire and you turn the magnet," I shrugged. "That's how an electric motor works."

"Exactly," he said patiently. "So electricity and magnetism are related to one another. Alter one and you alter the other.

They are Unified Fields."

"But that's not Einstein's Unified Field Theory, is it?" I asked.

Grandfather shook his head. "Einstein's Unified Field Theory adds another field. Gravity. You know what gravity is, don't you?"

I remembered my first lesson in gravity. It was when I was about seven. I was bouncing a ball in the back yard when my grandfather took the ball from me and told me to watch. He let it fall from his hand, it bounced a few times and then fell still. "Do you know why it did that?" he asked.

I shrugged. "I guess it just ran out of bounce like a car runs out of petrol?"

He shook his head. "No. Gravity did it. Gravity is a kind of invisible force. Think of it like a giant hand that pulls everything down."

That was a bit creepy! The idea of an invisible hand pressing me down haunted me for a week or so.

Grandfather used the ball as a model of the world to show how people could live underneath and still not fall off. After that, I spent a long time lying on my bed and trying to float. Something inside me told me that if I tried hard enough I could beat gravity and fly around the world.

Of course, no matter how hard I tried, I never did manage to float. I began to feel as if gravity was my enemy. I complained to Grandfather. "You're right!" he agreed. "Most of the time gravity is our friend – after all, it stops us falling off our Earth. But in some ways it seems like it's our enemy too. It stops us leaving the Earth and exploring the stars."

"Would you like to explore the stars, Grandfather?" I asked him.

"Any human with a gram of curiosity wants to know what's out there. Other planets and other peoples. So much knowledge."

So there and then, at seven years old, I decided I wanted to reach the stars one day. When I got a bit older, as I've already said, Grandfather explained the Unified Field Theory to me. After that we discussed it many times. Now, as I prepared to begin my school project, he coached me on how to present such a difficult concept to my class and teachers. He made it all sound so simple.

"Gravity is the force that holds us to the Earth," he began.

"Right. Now Einstein said that gravity was linked to electricity and magnetism. Three fields all linked – unified. You see what that means?"

I nodded and looked towards the setting sun. Behind me the purple sky was just dark enough for the first stars to appear. "Any change in electric force creates a change in magnetic force, and it also means that there's a change in the force of gravity. You can't change one without affecting the other. We can change an electric force – therefore, we can control gravity!"

Suddenly those stars seemed nearer.

"So why hasn't anyone done it?" I asked.

"Who says they haven't?" Grandfather said seriously.

"Is that what Einstein was doing during the War?" I asked.

"I think so," he said. "He came to the Naval Defence Research Committee to meet an old German professor called Ladenburg – another German who came to help us because he hated the Nazis. Ladenburg was an expert in mines and torpedoes – there was no secret about that. Everyone knew that Ladenburg was trying to find ways to protect our ships against German mines and their U-boat torpedoes. Imagine Albert Einstein's Unified Force Field surrounding a ship!"

I thought about it. "With a huge magnet and a vast power supply you might be able to create a sort of anti-gravity." I picked up a tennis ball from the back porch and bounced it. "A torpedo is attracted to a ship in the same way that this ball is attracted to the floor by gravity," I said. "And if the floor is protected by anti-gravity, the ball would be pushed up before it hit the floor. So maybe the torpedo would be pushed *away* from the ship."

"Correct," Grandfather nodded.

"But if they really did experiment with a ship," I argued, "it must have been a failure. Otherwise we'd have that sort of force field today."

"Well, perhaps," he said. "But maybe it wasn't exactly a failure. Maybe it just wasn't quite what they expected. Maybe it was *more* than they expected!"

"Go on!" I urged.

"Say they wanted to try this anti-gravity experiment," suggested Grandfather. "They'd almost certainly try it out on a model first, before risking it on a full-scale ship."

"That makes sense," I said.

"And I think that when they tried it on the model they discovered the force field had other effects. Not just anti-gravity, but something that would be equally as powerful if they used it in the War."

"Invisibility?" I asked. "So you were absolutely serious when you told me that a full-size warship became invisible?"

"There's a lot of evidence to suggest that it *did*. And I may have helped to make it happen!"

CHAPTER FOUR

By the now sun had disappeared below the horizon, but the sky was still light and the air mild so we sat there while Grandfather told me his part in the Philadelphia Experiment. "I was in my office at 8 am one morning and just contacting the computer by telephone..."

"I didn't know you had computers in 1943!" I broke in.

He chuckled. "A computer was a human being with a mind trained to do complicated maths problems very quickly. It wasn't one of those plastic boxes with a TV screen attached like you have in your room. Anyway, I was talking to my computer when my boss Doctor Anstrom looked through the window from the corridor and signalled that he wanted to speak to me. He said there was a meeting in the committee room and they needed a computer. I was the best they had in the building and he knew I could be trusted to keep quiet."

"What did you have to compute?" I asked eagerly.

He waved a pale hand at me and said, "Hold on, hold on, I'm coming to that. The first and most important thing is that when I saw the figures that they wanted me to work on, they were written in a curious spiral handwriting. I only ever saw one man write like that. Albert Einstein."

"I knew that Doctor Einstein wasn't there himself but it was plain he had written out the calculations for the committee to consider. Now, the other interesting thing was that these calculations were not to do with the Unified Field Theory that we had all guessed Einstein had been working on. They were to do with a force field surrounding a ship. But that force field wouldn't just deflect torpedoes around the ship – it would deflect light as well."

"You can't bend light," I said.

Grandfather said nothing. He signalled for me to stay

where I was, then rose and went into the house. A few moments later he came out holding a glass of water with a straw in it. He held the glass up to the pale sky and said, "What do you see?"

"A straw in a glass of water," I replied, stupidly.

"And what can you tell me about the shape of the straw?"

I sighed. I could see what he was getting at. "The straw is straight but it appears to be bent where it goes into the water."

"That's right. The straw is straight but the light waves coming from it are bent by the water. If a force field can twist gravity then it can twist light easily! Even a glass of water can twist light!" he cried.

"So the ship doesn't really disappear," I said slowly. "You just don't see it where it ought to be any more. You just see the sea. So where *do* you see the ship?"

He shrugged. "Somewhere else, I'd guess. And wherever that is, you could fire a hundred torpedoes at it but you'll never hit it because it isn't really there. It's like a picture on the television. Shoot at my picture on the television and you'll never scratch me – not if you shoot a million bullets at a million TV sets!"

"Amazing!" I said. "A new weapon. But did it work?"

"That's the million dollar question!" he said and spread his hands wide.

I slapped at his hand with my notebook. "You can't just leave it like that!" I said angrily. "There must be a proper ending to the story. I thought you said a warship disappeared?"

"It wasn't until a few years later that *that* story leaked out. When it did, of course I followed it with interest because I believed it was connected to the work I had done at the NDRC."

"So you never actually found out what happened to your calculations?" I asked.

"I handed them back to my boss, Dr Anstrom, and he didn't even say thank you. He went back into that meeting room, closed the door and I never heard any more about it."

"Didn't you tell anyone?" I asked. "I'd have told the newspapers – after the War, of course, when it wasn't a secret any more."

Grandfather sat down again and stared at the brightening stars in the purple sky. "No," he said quietly. His voice had changed; it was lower, more secret and more troubled. I'd never heard him sound this serious before. "There *are* some people who have talked about the disappearing ship – her name was the USS Eldridge, by the way. And as we all know, the project became known as the Philadelphia Experiment."

"So why don't *you* talk? The newspapers would probably pay you!" I smiled.

He took a deep breath and sighed. "Because the first man to talk about the Philadelphia Experiment met a strange death."

"He was murdered?" I breathed and suddenly I imagined shadows within the shadows of the garden wall.

Grandfather didn't answer directly. Instead he said, "Albert Einstein was a brilliant man, you know. He once said success is an equation, 'A = success. And A = x + y + z. Work is x, play is y and z is keeping your mouth shut.'" He looked at me. "Some people fail because they don't have 'z' in their lives. They just don't know when to keep their mouths' shut."

"Who would want to stop us talking about the Philadelphia Experiment nearly 60 years after it happened?" I asked.

He gave the slightest of shrugs. "Not the law enforcement people – not the FBI – maybe the spy people, the Central Intelligence Agency. I don't know."

"But *why* would they?" I persisted.

"Two reasons I can think of," Grandfather said quietly. "Either it all went horribly wrong and the government wants to hush up a story about its scientists killing our own sailors..."

"Or?"

"Or it was close enough to success for them to want to keep it secret. We may have someone out there now working on invisibility, or anti-gravity and we don't want the enemies of the USA to even guess what we might be up to." He sighed, and pinched his nose at the spot where his spectacles sat. He did that when he was worried. "Look, maybe you should just forget this idea of doing a project."

But I wasn't going to be put off. "This disappearing ship you were telling me about," I reminded him. "Did you see it – or not see it – yourself?"

"I didn't, no," he said quickly. "There were stories that went around later. Witnesses said USS Eldridge vanished but they could see the shape of the hull left in the water. I can understand that," he went on. "It's the other rumours that are strangest of all."

"Rumours?"

"Nothing more. Just wild stories. I'm not sure I believe them myself." He paused before continuing. "They reckon that not only did the Eldridge vanish from its yard in Philadelphia, it also appeared for a few moments at a dock in Norfolk, Virginia. It travelled hundreds of kilometres in the blink of an eye!"

I groaned. "So the Philadelphia Experiment could be about anti-gravity or it could be about invisibility or it could be about teleportation of matter. Great! Anything else?"

"Well," my grandfather said slowly. "There were some reports that the force field broke through the normal time-space continuum – that's how it appeared in two different places in a matter of seconds. It opened a sort of gateway into the rest of the universe. Some people even say the crew came across alien space travellers who use the same gateway to travel to Earth."

I rubbed my eyes. "Little green men?"

"Er, no. Little grey men, actually."

I stared at the glowing stars. The anti-gravity idea sounded worth following up. Even light bending was something I could investigate. But the rest was straight out of some old black and white movie. Could someone have been murdered to keep this secret? "Who was killed then, Grandfather? Who told the story of the Philadelphia Experiment?"

He turned and walked through the door into the house. "That's another story, Alice. Another story for another time. Right now it's time for supper."

Chapter Five

Grandfather kept me entertained that night by setting me a few problems of the sort he himself had been set back in 1943. With the help of my computer I solved them in half an hour. The computer I had at that time was just an IBM 286 – today's computers would make it look like a donkey cart in the Kentucky Derby, but it was still impressive. Back in 1943 my grandfather's brain had had to do the work of that computer. Now that was truly awesome!

My calculations certainly seemed to show that the force field really could bend light. I had another try at getting him to tell me the rest of the story of the Philadelphia Experiment, but he still refused. He said he wanted to dig out some old files and newspaper cuttings from the cellar and study them. He'd do that next day while I was at school and then, he promised me, he'd tell me the rest of the story.

School dragged along worse than ever that day. All I wanted to do was to get home so I could talk to Grandfather. When I was finally able to make my escape that afternoon I ran all the way home. I flung my bag on the floor of the hallway and hurried into the kitchen. He had an afternoon snack waiting for me – a glass of milk and a peanut butter sandwich. I almost choked as I tried to devour it in 30 seconds flat.

He simply raised a disapproving eyebrow as he watched me over the top of his glasses. I slowed down. I finished my sandwich, walked over to the sink and rinsed the glass and plate, then I sat down on a stool at the table.

"Good day at school?" he asked calmly.

"Same as ever," I said, impatiently.

"That bad, huh?"

I couldn't wait any longer. I leant forward. "So what have

you got to show me?" I asked eagerly.

He pointed to a range of files laid out on the table top. Each one had a label on the front with a name on it, written in capitals in his small, neat hand. "These are all files on scientists who've worked on electromagnetic fields," he began. He picked one up. "Men like Townsend Brown."

There was a faded photograph in the file of a thin man with deep, dark serious eyes. The file said he was born in 1905 and it listed his career through college and various jobs till he ended up in the Naval Research Laboratory in 1930. "That's where you worked, isn't it?" I asked.

Grandfather nodded. "Brown was older than me, of course – he was also in a different department. Plus, he was a very shy man. But we talked from time to time about some of his experiments. He was especially interested in gravity and came up with a box called a 'Gravitor' while I was there. The Gravitor seemed to prove that Einstein was right about the effects of electromagnetic force fields and gravity. He had a $50 million budget to spend and the government was right behind him. Then quite suddenly something changed. It all went wrong."

"And it was something to do with the Philadelphia Experiment?" I asked eagerly. "You think he could have been in charge of testing his work on the USS Eldridge?"

Grandfather shook his head. "We can't say that for sure. All I know is that in December 1943 Brown suddenly suffered a mental collapse and retired from the Naval Research Laboratory."

"But that doesn't prove he had anything to do with the Experiment," I said, disappointed.

Grandfather pulled out some handwritten notes. "I kept track of his career after the War. Townsend Brown seems to have really come up with some anti-gravity device. Just a model – a toy almost. A little silver disc that lifted off the ground and flew in a circle when it was charged with electricity. It could have meant a revolution in air travel –

space travel, even. Yet the reports just stated that he had failed to get financial backing."

"Nobody wanted his idea? Why?" I wondered. "You'd have thought people would be falling over themselves to get their hands on it!"

"Well, some people seemed to want the idea. Trouble was, something always happened to spoil things. One company showed an interest in Townsend Brown. Then, suddenly it was taken over by another company; and Brown lost his job. After that, a millionaire businessman came along and backed Brown. But the millionaire was killed in a mysterious plane crash. 'An accident' the report said carefully. Brown lost his job – *again*."

I picked up the notes and read them for myself. "He made enough money by 1958 to set up his own company," I said. "But he still couldn't find anyone to turn his models into full-size flying machines." I shook my head.

Grandfather turned to me. "Can you think of any reason why not?"

I took a deep breath. "I can think of three. One: Townsend Brown was unlucky. Some people are like that – everything they do goes wrong. Two: people had heard rumours about the Philadelphia Experiment and were afraid there'd be another disaster."

"And three?" Grandfather looked at me with a slight smile.

"Three: someone very powerful – the government maybe – didn't want Townsend Brown to succeed and they frightened off anyone who looked like they were going to support him."

"Good," Grandfather said. "Those are exactly the same conclusions that I came to."

"What happened to Brown?" I asked.

"Last I heard he was half-retired but still trying to sell his dream of anti-gravity to someone. Anyone."

I thought about this for a while. "Albert Einstein was working for the US Navy during World War II and he had a theory about anti-gravity. He worked with Professor Ladenberg – an expert on electromagnetic fields, and Townsend Brown was working in the same department on anti-gravity. Models were being tested, you were computing for their experiments and everything was going fine until late 1943. Then something happened. Something so disastrous the government has stopped research and won't even let anyone else carry on. What was it, Grandfather?"

He passed a file across to me. "Read that and decide for yourself," he said. "It's an amazing story. It only came out 15 years after the War. You have to make up your own mind if you believe it or not."

He left me with the file marked 'Jessup' and began preparing a bolognaise sauce for dinner.

I opened the file. And that's when I read for the first time the full, amazing story of the USS Eldridge.

CHAPTER SIX

Doctor Jessup was an interesting man who had nothing to do with the Philadelphia Experiment itself. He seemed an eccentric sort of a guy. A mathematician and an astronomer who somehow ended up exploring South American jungles.

While he was doing that he came across great ancient Inca buildings and was fascinated by them. Jessup decided there was no way that the huge stones could have been moved by men and llamas. They had to have had the help of some sort of anti-gravity device.

Anti-gravity device! Well, that was one link to the Philadelphia Experiment, but rather a loose one. Surely not enough of a link for the Navy to take a great interest in him? I read on. Doc Jessup also had an idea that anti-gravity machines may have been operated by ancient astronauts from space ships!

Another link, I thought. I remembered Grandfather talking about USS Eldridge breaking through some time-space barrier and encountering aliens.

Jessup wanted to investigate huge craters in the jungle that could have been made by landing spaceships. That was when he ran out of money and had to return to the USA. His jungle exploration was beginning to tie in with his other hobby – UFOs. There had been a lot of sightings in the late forties and early fifties and Jessup was taking them seriously. He wrote his book *The Case for the UFO* and published it to raise money. It was never a best-seller but it was popular enough with Ufologists, and Jessup made a few extra dollars travelling round the States talking about his theories.

Then, in 1958, he died. Jessup seems to have had the Naval Defence Research Committee worried. They had him watched and reported on. And they also seemed to know rather a lot about his death. The file held reports and a statement from the Navy.

The reports dwelt heavily on the fact that he'd been depressed at the time of his death. Apparently, his marriage had broken down and he'd also been involved in a road accident. He'd taken his car to a quiet road, they said, plugged a hose into the exhaust and led the other end into the car where he gassed himself with carbon monoxide. Verdict: suicide.

I felt the hair on the back of my neck begin to rise. There was something wrong here. Why was the Navy so anxious to emphasize the stories of Jessup's depression? They seemed to be trying just a little too hard to convince everyone that it was suicide.

But, if it wasn't suicide (and assuming he didn't accidentally plug a hose from his exhaust into his car window) then that only left one thing: murder. Like my Grandfather always said, 'Dead men tell no tales'.

"How are you getting along with that file?" Grandfather asked.

I looked up. "Do you think Jessup's death was suspicious?"

"Maybe. A lot of the people involved in the Philadelphia Experiment seemed to end up dead. It could kill you in two ways, I reckoned. If the force field didn't get you then the Navy agents would. No way out. But perhaps I'm being too suspicious."

"I can't see any connection between Jessup and the Philadelphia Experiment myself," I said. "OK, so he was into anti-gravity and believed aliens had the secret. But he wasn't anywhere near Philadelphia in 1943, was he?"

"No," Grandfather agreed. "But Carlos Allende was. And Carlos Allende read Jessup's books. And he decided Jessup was the best person to talk to about his experiences."

"Who's Carlos Allende?" I asked.

Grandfather nodded towards the file as if to say – "Read on and find out."

So I read on. And that's when I opened up a whole new can of worms.

Chapter Seven

While Doctor Jessup was travelling round the USA giving lectures on UFOs he received letters from all sorts of people. Some were scientists like himself, others ordinary people who had just become interested in the subject, and there were a few who sounded as if they might have been writing from cosy little cells with padded walls. Then one day he received a letter that was a scrawl of different colours. Maybe the writer had trouble holding a pen while confined in a straight jacket.

It was this writer who first drew Jessup's attention to an incident that happened in 1943 on the East Coast. I found a copy of this letter, neatly typed and turned into a thin booklet.

I guess that reading some typist's transcription loses the flavour of a letter written in coloured inks onto paper. Even so, Carlos Allende's letter to Jessup was wild enough for me to imagine the Doctor's reaction when he received it. I studied it carefully.

January 13, 1956

Doctor Jessup,

I read your book. I heard you give a lecture. You said that the USA should stop wasting money on developing 'rocket' travel to the stars, that instead we should look at Einstein's Unified Field Theory and develop 'anti-gravity' machines. You believe that there are forces that can lift huge objects into the air and that the Incas used them many thousands of years ago. I have to tell you Doctor, you are right. I have seen such things

with my own eyes!

We are told that Einstein never completed his theory. That's not true! He did complete it. But the things he discovered were so horrifying for mankind that he never published it. The Navy is now afraid to put the theory into practice. Why? Because it has already conducted a test and it was disastrous!

The result of the test was the complete invisibility of a ship – a destroyer – and all of her crew. This test was carried out in October 1943. The ship was wrapped in a force field of nearly a hundred metres across. Anyone inside the field could see vague shapes of other men on the ship but could not see the ship itself. They were walking on nothing. Anyone just outside the field could see the shape of the ship's hull in the water. Anyone further away would see nothing. The ship became invisible.

The disaster was that half the crew inside the field went as mad as hatters. Others seemed to be OK immediately afterwards, but later something strange began to happen to them. They would go blank and 'freeze' because they still had the effects of the field on them. Then the 'freezers' would disappear.

When this happened to somebody, it was vital that his ship mates marked the spot where he disappeared, went up to the spot and 'felt' for some skin – hands or face – to bring him back to this world. If they failed to reach him in time then he would burst into flames and disappear forever.

After 13 years there are few of the crew left. Many went insane. One walked through the wall of his cabin while his wife, children and shipmates watched. He was never seen again.

The Philadelphia Experiment was a complete success. The men were a complete failure.

Check newspaper reports in Philadelphia papers. They

report an incident where some sailors disappeared in a bar. The waitresses were so shocked they could scarcely put into words what they had seen.

Check the crew of the observation ship 'SS Andrew Furnseth'. The chief mate was called Mowsley and a crew member was called Richard Price.

Signed: Carl M Allen (Z416175)

PS:
1. The Navy did not know that the men would slip into invisibility after the Experiment was finished.
2. The Navy did not know that men would die when the field was switched on.
3. The Navy still does not know why it happened.
4. The Navy did not know that the crew would be able to walk through walls and disappear.

I should also mention that the ship later disappeared from its Philadelphia dock and appeared in its Norfolk dock a few seconds later. It was clearly identified in that place but then disappeared and returned to its Philadelphia dock. This was also reported in the newspapers but I cannot remember which ones.

Carlos Allende's letter was seriously weird, yet the more I thought about it, the more I felt that there could be some truth in it.

The writer was saying the Philadelphia Experiment began with tests for anti-gravity. That tied in with what Grandfather told me. It developed into an invisibility project and that's where my grandfather did the calculations for his boss.

But Allende's mention of side-effects on the crew was news to me.

If I believed Allende's letter to Jessup, then it suggested those side-effects could be pretty horrific. That might explain why the Navy had tried to stop Townsend Brown's work after the War.

Men dying, men going mad, men walking through walls and vanishing and worst of all, men 'freezing'. It seemed the 'freezers' vanished from sight yet they were still there. The only way to bring them back was to grope inside their shell of invisibility, touch their skin and draw them back into this world. If you failed then they burst into flames and vanished forever.

I closed the file as Grandfather served the bolognaise sauce on a bed of tagliatelle. He sat down at the table opposite me and picked up his fork. I did the same. But somehow I'd lost my appetite.

Grandfather watched me over the top of his glasses. "Do you see what I mean now Alice?" he said. "Even investigating the Philadelphia Experiment can be dangerous."

I nodded, then rested my forehead on my hands for a few moments while I turned the matter over in my mind. When I looked up, my face was serious. "I still want to try it!" I said. "I can't just stop here – there's so much more to unravel! Surely you want to know too? After all, you never even found out what happened to your calculations."

Grandfather thought for a moment and then said. "If you *are* going to continue, you'll need a certain amount of specialist information. Where are you going to get that information?"

I'd already thought about that. "There's a way of connecting my computer to the files of most of the big universities in the world. It's called a network – it works through the phone lines." I paused, then lowered my voice. "I've heard that you can even break into government files."

Grandfather sighed. "You don't know how," he said. "And I don't think it's such a good idea. You don't know what you might be getting into!" I could see he was torn between wanting to find out more and not wanting to stir up a hornet's nest.

"I'll learn. We can do it Grandfather. We can find out what really happened!"

"Or end up in a padded cell," he said.

"Or get a call from some government agents someday," I shrugged. "So what? I'll take that risk."

He pushed his food around his plate. "They don't come in the day," he warned. "They come at around 4 am when you're at your weakest."

I guess I knew at that point that Grandfather wasn't going to involve himself any more deeply in my investigations. I would have liked him to be in on it, but he'd made it clear he didn't want any trouble, and I had to respect him for that.

For me however, it was different. With the arrogance of youth, I'd made my decision, and now nothing was going to stop me. I was 16 years old and I knew what I wanted from my life. The same thing that Brown and Jessup and Ladenburg and Einstein himself had wanted. Knowledge.

CHAPTER EIGHT

After that, I really threw myself into my mission to discover the truth about the Philadelphia Experiment. I spent the next few years researching using whatever means I could. What began as a High School project became an obsession; I was determined to prove that Einstein's Unified Field Theory was possible. When I was just 16 years old, I gave up school to go to college. I was their youngest ever student. They had to let me in when I got 100% in the college entry tests – most students struggled to get 60%. But even they had nothing to teach me, and in the end I gave up college to concentrate on my research.

Grandfather helped with the maths calculations but he didn't have anything to do with my other activities. When I needed more information I raided the Naval research files by hacking into them. It was obvious that whatever information the Navy had on anti-gravity, they still considered it very secret – all the files were protected by 'Classified' codes. But they were no match for me. In time I became so skilled at hacking there was no code I couldn't crack.

Then, one day, I hacked into the Navy's latest research and to my complete astonishment, realized that someone was working along similar lines to me. Someone else was investigating the Philadelphia Experiment – and that someone had millions of pounds of government money behind them. Money set aside for a time when they might possibly recreate the Experiment. Greedily, I read the files, and as I did so a feeling of contempt began to grow inside me. They were making mistakes – mistakes that I could see right away. They were heading down a dead-end street and my maths brain knew it. It irritated me that they, with all their resources and support, were making what seemed to me like glaring errors. I was even tempted to hack into their files and tell them where they were going wrong! I resisted that temptation. I couldn't risk giving myself away, and anyway I didn't want them to succeed. *I* was going to be the one to solve the Philadelphia Experiment!

I think it was my hacking into those new files that first alerted someone to my illicit activities on the network. At any rate, it wasn't long after that that it happened. Grandfather's worst dream came true.

They came for *me*.

Chapter Nine

I don't know how long it took me to finish my story. I had told them quite a lot about myself, my life. I was pretty sure though that I hadn't told them *too* much.

There was silence for almost a minute. Then Agent Kirwan spoke. "We've looked at your school records," she said. That was her style. Direct and as blunt as the back of a Greyhound bus. But she had revealed that they *were* investigating me. "You were too bright for your teachers," she went on. The compliment did nothing to soften the blow.

"Yeah. I went to college when I was 16," I shrugged.

"Then you dropped out. Why was that, Alice?" Agent Miller asked.

"Because I didn't have time to follow the course. I knew all the stuff in the text books. I wanted to get on and do something revolutionary..." I stopped. There I went again, getting carried away! The trouble was, while they had obviously tracked me down, I still didn't know *exactly* what it was they were after.

I hesitated, unsure of what to say next. When my silence went on for five seconds Agent Kirwan jumped in and gave the game away. "Computer science. You were interested in computers," she urged.

Now the truth is that I am not very interested in computers. Computers are just a tool I use to achieve my aims. But if that was why they'd paid me a visit – well, I certainly wasn't going to argue. They'd handed me an excuse on a plate! "Yes, OK, I *am* interested in computers," I lied. I paused and tried to look defeated.

A quick look of triumph passed over the woman's face.

"So when did you begin stealing secrets from other

computers?" she asked. I took a deep breath. "Okay Agent Kirwan," I thought to myself. "I'll tell you what you want to hear. You've had more than enough chances to get at the truth, to unravel the bigger picture, and you've blown them all!"

I launched into my new personality of Alice Henreid – computer fan! "When I was at college, *everyone* was a hacker. We borrowed programs from other computer users..."

Agent Kirwan gave that odd soft snort again. "Borrowed! Stole, you mean!"

"All knowledge should be free. That's part of the hacker's ethic," I argued.

"Theft is theft. Someone spent a lot of time and a lot of money developing those programs. You just hacked into their systems and stole them."

"OK, OK." I said, holding up a hand.

"But recently you tried something a little different, didn't you Alice?" Agent Miller cut in. He had been silent for the last few minutes, and I'd almost forgotten he was there.

I groaned inwardly. Again, Miller was showing himself to be the cleverer agent. Should I admit it? And if I did, would I be admitting to something they didn't know about? A couple of seconds ago I was confident that I was going to get away with it. Now I wasn't so sure. I was aware that Miller was playing cat and mouse with me, and that I'd have to be on my guard. The last traces of sleepiness vanished, and I pulled myself upright in my chair. "I don't think so," I said.

Agent Kirwan blundered in again, "You have been traced hacking into the files of the Office of Naval Intelligence."

"Office of Naval Intelligence? You think I've hacked into your files?"

"We *know* you've hacked into our files."

This was it! They knew I was investigating the Philadelphia Experiment and now they were going to get me! They were going to confiscate my calculations.

Calculations more advanced than anything *they* had. I hung my head, expecting to hear Agent Kirwan's harsh, husky voice explaining my rights before she handcuffed me. But there was only silence I looked up at her, and she stared back, arms folded. My gaze travelled across to her partner, but he said nothing either. Both of them were looking at me expectantly, as if it were my turn to speak.

That's when I realized that they didn't know what I'd been doing at all. Sure, they knew I'd hacked into those files – but they had no idea *why*. How could they be so stupid? I tried not to let the relief show on my face, but inside I rejoiced. My confidence surged back. I was cleverer than they were! I even decided to play with them a little. I kept them waiting for an answer. Finally I said, "I did it just to see if it could be done."

That was it. That was what Agent Kirwan was after. I was nothing more than a clever youngster trying to beat the system. She straightened her back and gave me the lecture. I had committed a Federal offence, punishable by confiscation of all computer equipment – there could be a massive fine, possibly a spell in prison – think of the public shame for my grandfather...

I tried hard to look scared as her voice droned on and on. I think I even managed to squeeze out a tear or two!

"How could you honestly believe you could get away with it?" she finished. "We have ways of tracing computer hackers." She stared at me intently. "We're going to let you go – for now. But the matter is far from over. We'll be keeping an eye on you. Any further breach of Federal law and you'll be back here so fast your feet won't touch the ground. Understand?"

I looked up at her. "Yes, ma'am," I muttered. "Does that mean I can go?"

She rose to her feet and gave a brisk nod.

"Do I have to walk home?" I asked.

As she moved to the door she looked over her shoulder

and said, "Agent Miller will give you a lift."

"Thank you," I said as humbly as I could. Inside me, fireworks of celebration were going off. It was alright! They had simply brought me in to warn me, to frighten me off! I glanced at my watch and saw that it was 7 am. Grandfather would be getting up by the time I got home.

I was still celebrating inwardly when we pulled up outside the house. Right up to the moment when Agent Miller opened the door. "Right, Miss Henreid. Let's go and talk to your grandfather, shall we?" he said without warning.

All my smugness drained away in a second. "Grandfather? He knows nothing about my hacking!"

"No. But he knows about the Philadelphia Experiment, doesn't he?" the young agent asked. And those calm eyes showed an intelligence that I knew was almost equal to mine.

I led the way up the path swearing softly and viciously about the deviousness of men like Agent Miller.

Chapter Ten

Grandfather made us coffee and we drank it out on the porch. The coffee was scalding hot and it sharpened my brain again. I'd fooled Agent Kirwan. Agent Miller – the quiet one – was obviously going to be harder, but maybe there was still a way out. I decided to keep quiet until I knew what he wanted from me.

"I'm off duty now," he said, sipping carefully. "Anything you say to me will be off the record."

"I have nothing to say," I said.

Grandfather raised a hand. "Alice," he said, "I think maybe Agent Miller has something he wants to tell *us*." He turned to the man sitting beside him. "Do we have to call you Agent Miller when you're off duty?"

The young man grinned. "Charles – my friends call me Chuck."

"What do your enemies call you?" I scowled.

"Your invasion of Naval Intelligence files came through on a routine check and Agent Kirwan was assigned to deal with it. But I looked a little further. I saw a pattern in the hacking. I also looked up your family background and discovered exactly who Professor Henreid is. You are a highly respected scientist, sir," he said and practically bowed towards Grandfather.

Grandfather didn't speak, but nodded.

"Your granddaughter is also extremely clever."

"She's more than clever," broke in my grandfather, "She's brilliant!" He turned towards me, and his eyes were sparkling. But there was also a look in his eyes that I didn't recognize. It made me feel alone. "I know you're a loner, Alice, and I understand that. You take after me. But perhaps the time has come for you to share your skills with other people."

I said nothing, I was shocked Grandfather was saying this to me, but I waited for him to continue.

"I've been meaning to talk to you about something for a while now, and I've a hunch it might be the same thing that Agent Miller – Chuck – wants to talk to you about." He paused and cleared his throat. "Alice, you know how I always warned you that the Philadelphia Experiment was top secret, and that it was dangerous to mess around trying to investigate it?"

I nodded.

"Well, recently I've been thinking. Why can't you work on it from the inside? Governments need someone with your brain and you need the sort of money and equipment they have."

The agent put down his cup of coffee and closed his eyes for a few moments as if trying to come to a decision. Finally he said "Professor Henreid, you're a clever man. That's exactly what I wanted to speak to Alice about. There's just one thing..." He straightened in his chair. "You, sir, have been a loyal citizen of the United States for the whole of your life. I know I can trust you with classified information." He turned and looked me directly in the eyes. "But what about you, Alice? You said that hackers believe all knowledge should be shared freely. If I told you about certain classified files would you keep it to yourself?"

"Depends," I said cautiously.

"Classified files?" Grandfather asked. "Would they be the files about the the USS Eldridge? Are you saying that the story is true?"

"I'm saying that your granddaughter's work is valuable and perhaps, just perhaps, I can find a way to involve her in ongoing government research."

Grandfather nodded. "I'll cook us some breakfast and you can tell us more," he said.

CHAPTER ELEVEN

We went back into the house and while Grandfather busied himself at the stove, Agent Chuck Miller explained.

"Some of the Philadelphia Experiment files are so secret that agents like myself don't have access to them. The only people who see those Classified files are the President and some of his top advisers. All the hacking in the world won't get you into them. They're very old typed, even handwritten documents, kept in the world's safest strongroom. Come to work for the government and you may be allowed to see them yourself."

"You say you've never seen these files, but you must still know more about the Philadelphia Experiment than either of us," said Grandfather. He came straight to the point. "What exactly happened in 1943?"

"Well, like I said I've never actually seen the files but I believe what happened was that the NDRC did exactly what you suspect they did. They tried to apply Albert Einstein's Unified Field Theory without understanding just quite how powerful it really is. They blew a hole in time and space and let loose forces that we still don't understand after 50 years." He looked at me. "But if people like Alice work on it we may have the answers before another 50 years are over."

"I've read some of the latest research from several university records," I said. Then I added quickly. "It's all public knowledge, of course!"

Chuck gave a grin, "If you can understand it," he said.

"*I* understand it," I said. And I think the Philadelphia disaster makes sense."

"So, explain it to me!"

Grandfather put plates of ham and scrambled eggs in front of us and we sat round the table eating and talking. "It seems that the Unified Field Theory does not just link gravity, electricity and magnetism. It links everything in the universe. Once we understand Unified Fields we understand everything."

Agent Chuck Miller nodded. "Start changing electricity and magnetism and you don't just change gravity – you change light, space and even time."

"So time travel becomes possible?" Grandfather muttered.

"Time travel and space travel," I agreed.

"Can you explain to me how that's possible?" the agent asked. "Is it because anti-gravity allows you to travel at the speed of light?"

"No. It's because you can use gravity itself and shrink space to nothing." He still looked blank and even Grandfather was frowning. I picked up a sheet of paper and a pen. I wrote 'Proxima Centauri' on one end and 'Earth' on the other. Then I began to trace a line from one to the other. "What's the shortest distance between two points?" I asked.

"A straight line," Chuck said.

"OK. Here's Earth, and here's Proxima Centauri, our nearest star system. And this is a straight line between them. Travel along that line at the speed of light – that's 300,000 kilometres a second – and you'll reach Proxima Centauri in four years."

"We don't have rocket ships that can travel at the speed of light," Chuck said. "How long would it take in the sort of ships we do have?"

I did the calculation quickly in my head. "You'd get there some time after the year 28,000 AD."

"Her maths brain is as fast as a calculator," Grandfather grinned.

"Impressive," Chuck agreed. I tried to look modest.

"Anyway, there is a quicker way to get from Earth to Proxima Centauri," I said, picking up the paper. I folded it in half and slowly brought the words Proxima Centauri and Earth together. "The shortest distance between two points is not a straight line. The shortest way to get between two points is to fold space up like I folded this paper." I opened the paper and placed a finger on Earth. "Start on Earth, switch on a gravity field and fold up space – " I did this again with the paper. "Switch the gravity field off and you are four light years away with hardly any movement at all." My finger was now resting on the name Proxima Centauri.

Grandfather just nodded. Chuck asked, "But how?"

"Albert Einstein guessed a lot of this but he didn't have the kind of research that I've read in the past year or so. He didn't know that there are two sorts of Gravity – Gravity A and Gravity B. We know a lot about Gravity B because that's what keeps our feet on the ground and the Earth in orbit around the sun. But everything is made up of particles of matter. This table, for example," I said and rapped on it. "It's made up of billions of atoms and molecules and they're all held together by Gravity A. That's what scientists are exploring now. That's the secret of space travel, the secret of invisibility – maybe the secret of time travel."

"Invisibility and time travel?" the agent said. "You believe they are possible?"

"Scientists now *know* they are possible."

"How?"

"Scientists have measured the effects of gravity on light and time. You know that the sun sometimes moves between the Earth and certain stars. We know those stars are behind the sun—but we can still see them! The gravity of the sun is bending the light from the stars. Gravity can bend light. Bend it enough and you can wrap something in bent light and hide it from sight."

"So the Invisible Man could come true one day?" Chuck murmured half to himself. "What about time?"

"Take two devices that measure time. Place one at sea level where the Earth's gravity is strong and another on a mountain top where gravity is weak and they show different readings. Gravity twists time the way it twists light and space."

Agent Miller shook his head. He looked utterly overwhelmed. I allowed myself a satisfied smile.

CHAPTER TWELVE

Chuck had one more question. "There's a major part of the Philadelphia story that I just can't get my head around at all. It's this thing about the invisible men and the disappearing ship. What's the link?" he asked.

"I've just told you the link. Gravity! Remember the Unified Field Theory? If we can create an anti-gravity field then it affects time, space and light. When they did the Philadelphia Experiment, they used electricity and magnets to change gravity. They simply didn't realize that they were going to alter time and space as well. And, of course, they had no real control – nothing like the accelerator pedal and steering on a car. They just had an on/off switch. Imagine a car like that. Press the switch and you could go two kilometres an hour forward or 200 kilometres an hour sideways! No steering, no brakes!"

"Fine. But let's get back to 1943. What do you think happened?"

Grandfather leaned forward and rested his elbows on the table. It was his story about the vanishing ship that had first interested me in the whole idea. But now I realized I had overtaken him and knew more than he did. It was a frightening thought. I tried to explain calmly and clearly.

"The scientists at the NDRC fitted the USS Eldridge with a huge magnet and electrical coil. They then had two generator ships linked up to the Eldridge. A fourth ship had to stand off a kilometre out at sea to observe what happened. That was the ship Carlos Allende was working on. The men on USS Eldridge were supposed to be safe because they were inside the electromagnetic field. In fact they weren't."

"The Navy took a big risk with the lives of those men," Chuck said quietly.

"Big risk, sure. But if it had worked, the reward would have been bigger!" Grandfather cut in. "A force shield that could have ended the War in 1943 would have saved millions of lives. In wartime you sometimes have to take that sort of risk."

I continued with my explanation. "They threw the switch and the Unified Field Theory was proved right. The ship was surrounded by a powerful force field. A gravity field so strong that it bent the light and to the observers the ship seemed to disappear. But that gravity field did other things too. It folded up space," I picked up the piece of paper again, "so the ship went instantly to Norfolk, Virginia, 650 kilometres away. It also folded up time so it was seen in both places at practically the same moment. The crew members reported seeing alien spacecraft. That makes sense. If you imagine that the gravity field throws you onto a space-time highroad through the universe then you'd expect to meet other travellers on that highroad. If the crew were shocked by the sight of aliens then imagine what the aliens thought when they saw a huge warship hurtling past them!"

"How do you explain what's supposed to have happened to the crew?" Grandfather asked. "I know some went mad and threw themselves into the sea – I can understand that. But some didn't begin disappearing until weeks after the Experiment."

"I think that's to do with Gravity A – the gravity that holds this table together, and also holds our bodies together. If the crew had their atoms disrupted by the Philadelphia Experiment then their bodies would become unstable. They would be able to walk through walls the way you or I can walk through a mist. They could burst into flames or they could simply slip into another dimension. Now, we can actually see three dimensions, and we experience time as a fourth. But I've hacked into research from the 1980s on something called the super-string theory. That says there are ten dimensions – six that we humans can't see or experience."

Grandfather looked at me proudly. "So you can prove that the Philadelphia Experiment really happened!" he said.

"No. I can only prove that the Philadelphia Experiment *could* have happened – and *how* it could have happened. The real proof is still in a locked file somewhere," I sighed.

Agent Chuck Miller rose to his feet. "It's up to you, Alice. You can continue alone, working in total isolation, hounded by people like myself – or you can join the scientists working on these problems."

I toyed with the paper and looked at the words Proxima Centauri. A magical world that I might one day reach out and touch. "It's a tempting offer," I said.

"We need you, Alice. With your skill, your mind, you will one day be capable of opening every door that's ever been locked," Chuck said eagerly.

I liked the sound of that. And so did Grandfather. "Maybe he's right, Alice. You can go far. The sky's the limit."

I smiled and traced the words Proxima Centauri with my finger. "It's not often you're wrong, Grandfather, but you are this time. The sky's not the limit. There *are* no limits. No limits at all!"

GLOSSARY

CIA
(CENTRAL INTELLIGENCE AGENCY)
US agency set up in the late 1940s to protect the government from hostile foreign nations. The CIA employs agents in over 150 countries to send back information which it then assesses, offering its analysis to other US agencies. The CIA also attempts to prevent any risk to national security posed by foreign spies.

DIA
(DEFENSE INTELLIGENCE AGENCY)
Specialized US bureau employed in upholding government confidentiality and protecting its state secrets from potential trespassers.

FBI
(FEDERAL BUREAU OF INVESTIGATION)
Division of the US Justice Department, run from the national headquarters in Washington DC. The FBI is the most important investigating division of the government. Part of the Bureau deals with law enforcement and looks into federal crimes including kidnapping, espionage and treason. The FBI also gathers information on people or groups that could threaten national security.

NDRC
(NAVAL RESEARCH DEFENSE COMMITTEE)
Research wing of the American Navy. The NRDC devotes its studies to developing new weapons and devising top secret strategies to ensure US military supremacy.

UFO
(UNIDENTIFIED FLYING OBJECT)
An unexplained light or object that is either seen in the sky or detected on radar.

UNIFIED FIELD THEORY
Theory developed by the scientist Doctor Albert Einstein, which argues that gravity, magnetism and electricity are all inextricably linked. If this theory is correct, it could be possible for scientists to control gravity.

BIOGRAPHIES

This story contains fictional characters investigating a true-life mystery. Before you look at the facts and make up your own mind, here's a brief biography of the characters:

CARLOS ALLENDE
(ACTUAL CHARACTER
ALSO KNOWN AS CARL ALLEN)

Former sailor on merchant ship. Witness to an incident off the coast of the US when he says he saw a warship disappear. He knew Doctor Henreid and pieced together the facts surrounding the incident, which later became know as the Philadelphia Experiment. Allende wrote his suspicions in a letter to UFO book author Dr Morris Jessup, whom he later met and talked to.

TOWNSEND BROWN
(ACTUAL CHARACTER)

Scientist who developed anti-gravity devices but was never able to persuade people that they had any practical use. Either he was very unlucky – or someone was making sure his inventions were never a popular success.

DOCTOR ALBERT EINSTEIN
(ACTUAL CHARACTER)

One of the world's greatest mathematicians. Some of his theories explained the whole foundation of time, space and the universe. Some also had practical uses – one of his theories led to the creation of the atomic bomb and nuclear energy. His ideas about a Unified Field Theory, presented in 1953, were never completed, but work is still going on which could have practical use in military defence systems – like the Philadelphia Experiment?

ALICE HENREID
(FICTIONAL)

Granddaugther of brilliant mathematician Joseph Henreid, who shares his enthusiasm and expertise for science and maths. Uses her computer hacking skills in an attempt to discover the truth about the Philadelphia Experiment.

DOCTOR JOSEPH HENREID
(ACTUAL CHARACTER, DISGUISED NAME)

Mathematician and former adviser to US Naval Defence Research Committee. He worked on problems related to Albert Einstein's Unified Field Theory. He believed those calculations may have been used for force field experiments but he was not told anything about the Philadelphia Experiment.

DIA AGENT KIRWAN
(FICTIONAL)

Investigator for the DIA, working to protect the US government from possible leaks or espionage that could threaten national security. Kirwan mistakingly believes that Alice Henreid's forays on the computer are merely the random movements of a young hacker.

DOCTOR MORRIS JESSUP
(ACTUAL CHARACTER)

Astronomer and later scientist in the service of the US Government. He became interested in UFOs after a trip to South America and devoted his career to documenting alien encounters. Jessup became involved in the Philadelphia Experiment after receiving a letter from Carlos Allende, and died in mysterious circumstances.

DIA AGENT MILLER
(FICTIONAL)

Kirwan's colleague and the more intuitive of the two agents. Miller realizes that Alice is hacking in order to achieve a distinct goal — to access government records about the Philadelphia Experiment. He believes that if she is loyal to the US government, the authorities could use her phenomenal mind to officially study in this field.

CLASSIFIED FILES

Did it really happen? Could a ship really disappear? The Navy has never admitted conducting the Experiment, and the classified files have never been opened. But there are some pieces of evidence worth considering:

The Philadelphia Experiment DID happen because

There is a secret film. An electronics engineer, 'Dave', reported a conversation with a security guard whose name he remembers only as 'Jim'. Jim said that in 1945 he'd been working as a guard for a secret film store. One day he found he was in a position to watch a film being shown to high ranking naval officers. This black and white film showed an experiment being performed at sea. While his guard duties did not allow Jim to watch the whole film he was able to see snatches of it. There was no commentary on the film, but it showed three ships. Two of the ships seemed to be feeding energy waves into a third ship. These, Jim thought, could have been sound waves. After a time the ship in the centre, a destroyer, disappeared slowly into a transparent fog so that all that was left was the imprint of the ship in the water. When the energy waves were turned off the ship reappeared. Jim overheard some of the conversations among the officers. Some were claiming the energy had been left on for too long and this had led to problems for the crew members. One officer said that some crewmen later disappeared while drinking in a bar, some were:

not in their right minds and never would be
and some disappeared without trace.

BUT:

It would be difficult to ever trace Jim because his surname is not given. And, if the Navy considered the Philadelphia Experiment to be such a big secret that it was worth covering up for 50 years, would they really allow a guard to see such a film – or overhear the officers talking?

There was a possible eyewitness. Two airmen were walking in a park in Colorado Springs when a stranger approached one of them and told them a strange tale. He claimed he'd been a naval officer but was sacked because he had gone 'crazy' as the result of an experiment. When one of the airmen asked about the experiment, the stranger said it involved invisibility. It worked perfectly on the ship they were using but the force field they used had a harmful effect on the minds of the crew. The stranger said it happened in Philadelphia and it involved electrical energy fields. He claimed that some of the crew saw double, while others said they had been transported to another world where they'd talked to alien beings. Some recovered, some died and some went mad. The Navy dismissed the crew on the grounds of mental illness – thereby ensuring that they would not be believed if they ever repeated the story of the Philadelphia Invisibility Experiment. The airmen never saw the stranger again.

BUT:

The story cannot be checked because no one knows the name of the stranger. Why has this strange man not told his fantastic story to anybody else? If the sailors really were made ill by an experiment, then wouldn't the Navy treat them? Or if they couldn't be cured, wouldn't it at least lock them away rather than let them roam the world spreading the story of the secret experiment?

A photocopy of a newspaper cutting has been found. The newspaper reports mentioned by Carlos Allende in his letter to Jessup have never been traced, but a photocopy of a newspaper clipping has come to light. There is no date on it and there is no clue as to where it came from, however it does seem to back up Allende's story. It reads:

Strange Circumstances Surround Tavern Brawl

City Police Officers were called to help Navy Shore Patrol officers in breaking up a tavern brawl near the Navy Docks here last night. They got something of a surprise when they arrived at the scene to find the place empty of customers. According to a pair of nervous waitresses the Navy Shore Patrol had arrived first and cleared the place out. But not before two of the sailors did a remarkable disappearing act. "They just sort of disappeared into thin air – right there!" said one of the scared waitresses, "and I ain't been drinking either!" At that point, she said, the Navy Shore Patrol hustled everybody out very quickly.

One reported witness dismissed it as "a lot of hooey from them daffy dames down there" and claimed it was all a publicity stunt to attract visitors. Police confirmed that there had been a brawl resulting in $600 of damage but would not comment on the strange disappearances.

If genuine, then it seems a convincing
newspaper report suggesting that the Navy's
own shore patrol knew about the Philadelphia
Experiment and the problems of disappearing
men, and hurried to the scene to clear all
witnesses out before the police or press
arrived.

BUT:

The original newspaper article has never
been traced. It would be easy to fake a
newspaper report, photocopy it and send it to
investigators. No one knows who sent the
clipping. The columns of the printed report
are too wide for it to have come from any
1940s Philadelphia newspapers.

The official records have gone
conveniently missing. Carlos
Allende claimed to be
a crew member on the
SS Furuseth and signed himself Z416175 in
his letters to Doctor Jessup. The crew records
of the SS Furuseth show that crew member
Z416175 was certainly aboard in October
1943 when the Philadelphia Experiment took
place. His name is given as Carl Allen – one
of the names Carlos Allende used. The
problem is that the records of the
disappearing ship, USS Eldridge, have been
lost. The Navy says they are 'missing'. Very
convenient if they are trying to cover up a
disastrous experiment! There is no record,
then, of the ship being used for experiments.

There is no evidence that she was ever in the same area as Carlos Allende's ship. Could Carlos Allende have seen the USS Eldridge? The official records show that the USS Eldridge was in Bermuda in October 1943 – so Carlos Allende must have been lying. However, there are other wartime records including some called 'action records'. These show that the ship was off the coast of North Africa in November 1943 – in the same convoy as Allende's SS Furuseth! The official records were either mistaken, or had been deliberately changed to hide the truth.

BUT:

False records don't prove that the USS Eldridge was involved in the Philadelphia Experiment. They may have been invented to hide the fact that she was engaged on some other kind of secret trials – mine detecting, for example.

Experiments have proved that electromagnetic force fields really can harm people. In 1976 some classified documents were released to the public. They gave details of experiments conducted in the USSR; these experiments looked at the effects of electromagnetic force fields on the human organism. The Soviet scientists discovered that these force fields really did affect the brains and the bodies of people exposed to them. They suffered:

disturbances to their nerves and their blood circulation as well as **dizziness, forgetfulness, loss of concentration, anxiety and depression.**
BUT:

The experiments did not use the immense force field power needed to make a warship disappear, neither did they make the victims disappear, walk through walls or burst into flames. Humans are often surrounded by electromagnetic force fields but no one has ever complained of vanishing.

It is known that there *were* secret projects concerning warfare at sea. In 1943 the USA was involved in a bitter sea war in the Pacific against the Japanese Navy. They would have tried almost anything to give them an advantage against the enemy. In Europe the British inventor Geoffrey Pyke mixed water with wood pulp, froze it solid and created an incredibly tough material called Pykrete (Pyke-concrete). Bombs and shells would bounce off it. He suggested that the US and British Navies build a fleet of aircraft carriers from the stuff. He even wanted teams of commandos to spray enemy factories with Pykrete so they would be frozen out of action. British Admiral Mountbatten caught Prime Minister Winston Churchill in his bath and dropped a lump of Pykrete in. It didn't melt. Churchill ordered more tests and a Pykrete ship sailed through a long hot summer on a Canadian lake without melting. In the end, Germany was defeated before the Pykrete fleet was built. It's an example of an idea that sounds crazy but was taken seriously at the time. So, what's so unusual about trying an invisibility project? In 1996 manufacturers were building Stealth aircraft that are 'invisible' to enemy radar. Is that the sort of invisibility that the US Navy was trying to achieve in 1943? And did a tragedy result from the Experiment? Is that why the Navy refuses to talk about the Philadelphia Experiment?

Force Fields

Have you ever had a dream where you find
yourself flying? A dream where you soar
over houses and fields, over seas and
mountains? Like a magic carpet from some
tale from the Arabian Nights? Will it always
be just a dream? Or is it possible?
Imagine a ray that can pass through your body
and come out of the other side without harming
you. A hundred years ago most people would
have said that was as foolish as a magic carpet
ride. Then, in 1895, Wilhelm Konrad Roentgen
was experimenting with tubes that gave out
coloured light and noticed that some of the light
rays passed through a sheet of cardboard. He
had discovered X-rays – by accident!
Twenty-five years later a young scientist
called Townsend Brown was experimenting
with X-ray tubes because he believed they
might hold the secret of space travel. He
believed that they could have a force of their
own. When he switched on an X-ray tube he
could sense that the whole tube seemed to
have a thrust as if it were trying to move.
After many experiments he discovered that
the X-rays didn't have the power to move
things. It was the high voltage electricity that
was causing the thrust. He built a small
plastic box with a high voltage tube inside –
he called it a 'Gravitor'. When it was

switched on it lost about one per cent of its weight. It was cancelling out gravity!

Imagine a Gravitor under your carpet. If you could turn the weight-loss up to 100 per cent then you'd be floating. Up to 101 per cent and you'd start to rise. At 200 per cent you'd be rocketing away from Earth as quickly as you'd fall down from the top of the Eiffel Tower! A truly magical carpet, but with science taking the place of magic.

Doctor Henreid met Townsend Brown at the Naval Research laboratory meetings.

Townsend Brown could have been involved in the Philadelphia Experiment, but there is no proof of this. His work was a classified secret. However, there are some strange questions surrounding his life and work. You can make up your own mind about the answers:

 Townsend Brown was working for the Navy but was sent home to rest in December 1943.

He had suffered a nervous collapse. This was shortly after the Philadelphia Experiment had allegedly been carried out. Did the failure of the Experiment bring about his nervous collapse? Or was the failure so great that the Naval Research Laboratory blamed him and dismissed him?

After the war Townsend Brown became extremely interested in Unidentified Flying Objects and he suggested that scientists should look into the way UFOs can fly. He said that if the government put money into his Gravitor research he might be able to come up with the answer! Why did the government refuse? Had they seen the disastrous effects of electromagnetic force fields in the Philadelphia Experiment?

In 1952 Townsend Brown's Gravitor was so powerful that it could lift more than his own weight. He went on to power disc-shaped models that could fly at 19 kilometres an hour round a six metre diameter circular course. They gave off a slight hum and a bluish glow, just like the 'flying saucers' of so many UFO reports. The models were so spectacular they were immediately classified as secret. But the government still didn't develop the idea. Had they had contacts with alien visitors? Have these aliens already passed on the secrets of anti-gravity power?

Townsend Brown was so sure his ideas could change the world that he went to Europe to sell Gravitor power to France. A company supported his research but was taken over by another company. The new company stopped his experiments. He returned to the USA where a rich backer helped him. The rich backer died mysteriously when his aeroplane

crashed into an overhead power cable –
mysterious, because the pilot was too
experienced to make such an elementary
mistake. Was the French take-over arranged
by someone trying to stop Townsend Brown?
Did Brown's enemies even go so far as to
murder his rich backer?

Imagine being free of gravity at the turn of a
switch. A scientist called Townsend Brown
has come close to making the magic real.
Why can't we have our magic carpets?
Remember the invention of X-rays a hundred
years ago. In time it was found that some of
the radiation from them could seriously
damage a patient's health if it wasn't
controlled properly. Has someone decided that
the Gravitor forces are too dangerous? If so,
who? How do they know? Have they
conducted a real test? And was that test
known as The Philadelphia Experiment?

Unlocking the Classified Files

The US Navy has always denied that there was
ever a Philadelphia Experiment – or any sort of
invisibility tests in 1943 or at any other time.
Many of their files are classified as secret. In
this story we have assumed that there is a
way to get into those files. Through hacking.
When computers became available to
everyone in the 1970s it wasn't long before
valuable information began to be stored on
them. And it wasn't long before computer
hackers found ways to gain access to those
files and the secrets they contained. Large
business computers rarely stand alone. They
are linked to other computers by telephone
lines – and those lines send information and
receive information. They are the doorway to
let someone into the computer. And that
person might be a hacker.
In the 1960s and 1970s the word 'hacker'
meant someone who simply explored the uses
of computers and developed new programs. By
the 1980s it had taken on a new meaning. It
was now someone who could steal into another
computer like a burglar steals into a house.
And, like burglars, the hackers could vandalize
what they found there or steal it. In fact, most
hackers merely took a copy of what they found
there, so the owners of the computers didn't
even know they'd been burgled!

THE HACKERS

The earliest form of hacking was known as 'phreaking'. This was a way of making telephone calls to all parts of the world without paying. One way was to dial a 0800 Freephone line, wait till the recorded message was finished and listen for the dialling tone. Using a new code number the phreaker could then dial any number, anywhere in the world, and the bill would go to the Freephone company – not the phreaker. Later, electronic dialling boxes ('blue boxes') were built and sold to computer hackers who wanted to connect to company computers and hack into them for free. The first blue box was confiscated by police in 1961.

Hackers need an address-number to contact a company computer. Many of these addresses are published by phone companies – others are shared among hackers. Companies wishing to keep some information secret will use a password. When you try to read some information the company will ask you for the password – if you don't know it then you don't get the information. The trouble is many operators are really lazy about passwords. One company was worried that it was losing secrets and had its system checked. The experts found that 61 passwords were simply AAAAAA – though two had been changed to BBBBBB! Others included OPEN SESAME and 30 were first-names of people using the system. Some operators forgot their passwords so they stuck them onto the computer monitor where anyone could see them. No wonder hackers can break into classified files – computer operators give them the keys!

Secrets are often left for other computer users to read. They are left in files called bulletin boards. Many of these have shocked governments, police forces and the public. Information left on bulletin boards has included 'Ten ways to kill a cop', 'How to manufacture tear gas', 'A guide to shoplifting without being caught' and 'What to carry in a riot'. A step-by-step guide to making plastic explosives was on a bulletin board operated by a fourteen-year-old school boy.

Not all hackers get away with their activities. A hacker in Birmingham, England, fell in love with a policeman's daughter. He hacked into a florist's computer and sent her three bouquets of flowers every day – at no expense to himself. By the end of the week the house was full of flowers and the irritated policeman investigated. The hacker was caught.

Some hackers see themselves as 'Robin Hood' characters, fighting for freedom against the authorities. In Scotland a group of hackers claimed they had robbed the rich to help the poor. They hacked into a local tax system known as the Poll Tax. Every two weeks the names of poor tax payers would be taken off the tax lists and replaced by the names of people who had died. The council was worried about the money it could lose in this way. However, it seems likely that the story of this hack was invented. Hackers *could* have carried it out – but they didn't.

Hackers who plan to make vast sums of money from their crimes can get into bank accounts and simply transfer millions of pounds across to their own account. In 1989 a London company discovered it had lost £50 million in this way, although they did manage to recover it. An American group had a more ingenious scheme. They changed bets in bookmakers' computers so they were able to bet on a horse race after it had finished. Naturally, they won. They earned several million dollars before they were finally arrested.

A British Hacker, Edward Singh, couldn't afford a computer or phone lines. So he walked into Surrey University Computing Unit and used their machines. Everyone thought he was a student. It was only when an American hacker was caught that the US authorities learned about Singh's activities. They invited him to America to 'talk' about his skills – it was in fact a plot to arrest him! In the end he was arrested by British police, but they had very little to charge him with. He admitted getting into some of the most secret military information, but said he'd found it boring. In the end he was released without being charged. The US authorities were not happy about that.

Catching hackers takes a lot of skill and cunning. Dr Clifford Stoll, an astronomer in a Californian laboratory, came across a small example of hacking into his company's files. He traced the activities of the hacker and discovered he had hacked into American Air Defence systems, chemical and nuclear weapon plans, the Space Shuttle Program and the US President's files. Stoll set up a completely fake set of files on the Star Wars Space Defence Program, knowing that sooner or later the hacker would want to sample it. Like a mouse tasting cheese in a trap the hacker broke into the phoney files. Stoll was ready with tracking equipment and traced the address of the hacker in West Germany where he was arrested.

How far can computer hackers get into top secret national programmes? In April 1986 hackers interfered with the US Space Program computers. They were able to change the course of a satellite in its orbit around the Earth. Could that sort of hacker break into Naval Intelligence files and steal Philadelphia Experiment secrets? What do you think?

ALBERT EINSTEIN

Einstein's Unified Field Theory lies at the heart of the Philadelphia Experiment, but the great scientist himself is probably just as mysterious as his fantastic theories. Much of Einstein's work remains unchallenged, even incomprehensible to most scientists today. And many modern scientists believe that Einstein's pursuit of 'order' in this chaotic universe, is a largely unobtainable goal. But his new conceptions of time, space, mass, motion and gravitation – Relativity – revolutionized the scientific world. He proved that matter and energy are interchangeable. His famous equation $E=MC^2$ (energy equals mass times the velocity of light squared) became the basic theory behind the development of nuclear energy.

Although he evoked terrible consequences by splitting the atom, Einstein was actually a pacifist. He worked relentlessly for world peace. But he feared the might of Nazi Germany. As a result, he wrote a letter to President Roosevelt in 1939, in which he outlined the possibilities of building an atomic bomb. Einstein was concerned that Germany might create the atomic bomb first and if they did, the results would be horrific. As a consequence of Einstein's scientific work and his urging, and of course the work of Dr J. Robert Oppenheimer, the US finally achieved production of the atomic bomb in 1945. Its use brought about the end of World War II. Einstein's reaction to the atomic age would have been mixed as he had always questioned the morality of using scientific developments for self-destructive purposes. His personal secretary, Helen Dukas, recalled his response in her book *Albert Einstein, Creator and Rebel:* **when the bomb was exploded over Hiroshima his worst fears were realized. His horror of the bomb whether in dictatorial or democratic hands, weighed heavily on his conscience.** But Einstein's Theory of Relativity did not fully satisfy him. As a result he turned his attention to the Unified Field Theory. Relativity did not include the other dynamic of electromagnetism, which really excited the scientist. He spent the last 25 years of his life working on it.

While it cannot be absolutely proven that Einstein was involved in The Philadelphia Experiment, records *do* show that Einstein was in fact in the employment of the US Navy as a scientific consultant from May 31, 1943 to June 30, 1944. However the exact nature of his work has never been disclosed. There is much debate as to whether or not Einstein finished working on the Unified Field Theory. Certainly, Einstein himself felt that if he could not show that a theory was possible, then perhaps nobody could. The question remains, was The Philadelphia Experiment a failed attempt at completing the Unified Field Theory? Or even a successful one?

THE MYSTERIOUS DEATH OF DR JESSUP

Is the US Navy seriously worried about people uncovering facts about the Philadelphia Experiment?

Doctor Morris Jessup was the first man to give wide publicity to the Philadelphia Experiment. He died in a car filled with exhaust fumes. The police decided it was suicide. But was it? Could it have been murder? Maybe Naval Intelligence decided to silence Jessup once and for all. What evidence is there that Jessup's death was suspicious?

It is state law in Florida to hold an autopsy on the body of a suspected suicide. The body is dissected by a doctor and all possible causes of death explored. There was no autopsy performed on Jessup and no reason given for the law being broken.

The body was tested for alcohol and for carbon monoxide poisoning. Some reports say there was no alcohol but the blood was saturated with carbon monoxide from the exhaust fumes as you would expect. But no tests were carried out for drugs. Dr Jessup could have been drugged, placed in the car and the hose connected to the exhaust.

Another report says there *was* alcohol in Dr Jessup's blood. In fact there was so much alcohol that he could not possibly have driven the car to the suicide spot, connected the hose to the exhaust and climbed back into the car. He must have had help from someone. Someone who wanted him dead?

Mrs Jessup refused to identify her husband's body, claiming she was too upset. She kept repeating, **It can't be my husband, it can't be my husband!** The man who identified the body was named as Leon Seoul. No one has been able to trace this Mr Seoul since. Did Leon Seoul ever exist? Was the body Dr Jessup's at all?

The body of the suicide was examined by Dr Harry Reed, according to police reports. Harry Reed was walking through the park when the police dragged the body out of the car and tried to revive him. Dr Reed declared the victim dead at the scene. But no one has since been able to trace any doctor called Harry Reed in the state of Florida. Another invention to cover up the truth? Or a doctor paid by the killers, not to revive Jessup, but to check that he was dead? And why was the doctor walking through the park when it was closed for the night?

People who commit suicide usually leave a note explaining their actions. There is no police record of any note being found in Jessup's home or in the car.

The suicide attempt was very professional. Back windows of the car had been sealed with dampened clothing – even though there was no water for 180 metres. Had Jessup carried damp towels all the way from home? The washing machine hose attached to the exhaust was wired into place. It was likely that the preparations took place in daylight just a short distance from a busy road. Surely someone would have seen him?

All of these facts make the suicide look suspicious

BUT:

1 Doctor Jessup had been very depressed by his divorce
2 His new books were being rejected by publishers because they were not good enough
3 Scientists were criticizing his UFO ideas and refusing to take him seriously
4 A serious car accident had stopped him from working

5 Although he left no suicide note, he had written a depressed letter to a friend saying **another existence or universe may be better than this miserable world**

6 He had previously asked for his body to be used in medical research. An autopsy would have meant that his organs would have been useless for that purpose. Maybe that's why the authorities didn't perform one

If the Navy hoped to murder Jessup and stop inquiries into the Philadelphia Experiment then it all went disastrously wrong for them. Jessup's strange death made people more interested in his work, not less – and books were written to show that it proved he was on to something important and secret.
Then an investigation was carried out by a writer called James R. Wolfe. Wolfe was convinced that the Philadelphia Experiment was being covered up. He said the Navy was not worried by the damage the truth would do to them. The Navy was worried about the damage it would do to a famous and powerful individual.
Who was this individual? What had Wolfe discovered about the Jessup suicide/murder? We'll never know.
Before his findings were published Wolfe disappeared!

THE SURVIVOR'S STORY

Carlos Allende (or Carl Allen) was the first witness of the 1943 Philadelphia Experiment to come forward. He knew Doctor Henreid, a man who had done Unified Field Theory calculations for the Navy during World War II. Doctor Henreid was a respected scientist — even today his real name cannot be revealed. Carlos Allende said he'd witnessed the Philadelphia Experiment on USS Eldridge from a near-by ship.

The second witness was the unknown sailor, who talked to two airmen and claimed to be a survivor from USS Eldridge. But he gave no name, so he could never be traced. Perhaps the airmen could even have invented him.

The most convincing story would be one from a known survivor — preferably one who was on board the USS Eldridge. And such a witness has come forward. His name is Alfred D. Bielek.

By the late 1980s most investigators had decided there would be no new Philadelphia Experiment evidence until the Navy opened its classified files. Then, in Phoenix, Arizona in 1989, there was a UFO conference. A man called Alfred D. Bielek stepped forward and told the members of the conference that he had survived the Philadelphia Experiment.

Alfred D. Bielek said he had been made invisible and had travelled through space–time warps and lived to tell the tale. Here is his story:

In 1939 two specialists in physics, Edward Cameron and his half-brother Duncan, were invited to join some force field experiments. These had been going on since as early as 1931 under the code name 'Operation Rainbow'.

In 1940, three years before the Philadelphia Experiment, they took part in an experiment where a small ship was made invisible. No one was on board the ship when it disappeared so no one was hurt.

There was a larger experiment on a battleship in March 1942, however it failed. Edward Cameron believed that this was because the scientist in charge was worried about the harmful effects of electromagnetic fields, and therefore sabotaged the experiment. The scientist in question, Tesla, left the project. Ten months later he was found dead in his New York hotel room.

The next test was on the USS Eldridge. It was fitted with invisibility generators and in July 1943 it was switched on. Edward Cameron and his brother were below decks looking after the equipment. They survived, but most of the crew above decks went insane.

A second USS Eldridge test was attempted in August of the same year. This time the ship vanished for four hours. Edward Cameron saw maddened crew men jump overboard. But they did not land in the sea — they landed on the grass outside a Long Island army base, 40 years in the future, in 1983.

Cameron noticed that a flying saucer was also 'sucked' though the gap the experiment had apparently blown in time. The flying saucer also ended up in 1983. Edward Cameron believed the UFO had been trying to warn them of the dangers of their force field experiments.

The final experiment was on October 27, 1943. This was the one witnessed by Carlos Allende and the one that became known as the Philadelphia Experiment. The USS Eldridge crew went mad or found themselves embedded in the steel of the ship where they burst into flames. Again, Edward Cameron and his brother were saved by being below decks.

After this last experiment, the brothers began to make a fuss about the dangers of playing about with force fields. They were 'dealt with' by a secret government agency. Their bodies were destroyed and their souls were transmitted into new bodies.

Edward Cameron's memories were washed from his brain and he was placed in the body of Alfred D. Bielek. But when Bielek saw the 1988 movie of the Philadelphia Experiment, it stirred up what traces of memories were left in his brain. He began to remember that he wasn't Alfred D. Bielek born in 1927 — he was scientist Edward Cameron born

August 4, 1916. All record of Edward Cameron has been destroyed by the government. There is now no proof he ever existed.

Since that date Alfred D. Bielek has been investigating the Philadelphia Experiment and remembering lots of new details. His brother was less fortunate; his transfer to a body born in 1951 went wrong; he suddenly began to age one year for every hour and died of old age in three days.

Alfred D. Bielek (or Edward Cameron, if you believe his story) now thinks that the invisibility project which started in 1931 was not set up by Earthly scientists. It was set up by aliens who looked almost human. In fact, he says these aliens are still around and are moving freely amongst us. They bleach the green tint from their skins and pass themselves off as humans. The whole point of the Philadelphia Experiment was not to give Earthlings an invisibility shield — it was to blast that hole in time-space so the aliens could travel through time-space easily.

The aliens are not truly evil, Alfred D. Bielek says. They are just the servants of an even more powerful alien race of reptiles.

Can we believe this staggering story? It seems incredible, but Alfred D. Bielek has convinced many people. You will have to make up your own mind whether or not you believe him.

Einstein's attempt to write a Unified Field Theory is undeniably a fact.

Scientists could well have conducted experiments to test the forces that he suggested were involved. Light can be bent and simple anti-gravity machines have been built. They may have been tested on a ship with catastrophic results.

But a government agency that can transmit your soul into another body? Aliens who bleach their skins and pretend to be humans? Reptiles who really control the world? What do you think?

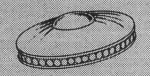

EPILOGUE

The US Navy insists that the Philadelphia Experiment never took place. That it is nothing but a legend dreamed up by madmen who live in a world of fantasy. The Navy's Public Enquiries Section has a standard letter it sends out to anyone who asks about the Philadelphia Experiment. It says:

Dear Sir/Madam,

Over the years we have received innumerable queries about the so-called 'Philadelphia Experiment' or 'Project'. These queries increase every time the subject is mentioned in the press or in a science fiction book.

The legend dates back to a book called *The Case for UFOs* by the late Dr Morris Jessup. Some time after the publication of the book Doctor Jessup received a letter from Carlos Allende giving details of an alleged secret experiment in Philadelphia in 1943. According to Allende a ship was rendered invisible and teleported to and from Norfolk in a few minutes with some terrible after-effects for the crew members. Supposedly this incredible feat

was accomplished by applying Einstein's never-completed 'Unified Field Theory'. Allende claimed he had witnessed the experiment from another ship and that the incident was reported in a Philadelphia newspaper. Neither the identity of Allende, nor that of the newspaper has ever been established.

The office of Naval research has never conducted any investigations on invisibility either in 1943 or any other time. In view of present scientific knowledge, our scientists do not believe that such an experiment could be possible except in the realms of science fiction. A scientific discovery of such importance could hardly remain secret for such a long time.

I hope this provides a satisfactory answer to your enquiry.

Well? Does it provide a satisfactory answer to YOUR enquiry?

Or do you wonder why, if there's nothing in the story, they won't open up their files on the subject?

Afterword

by Robert Irving

I first got wind of the Philadelphia Experiment while out at night making crop circles; as one of many tales we'd tell to get us in the mood. It was dark and spooky, and perfect. **There are more things in heaven and Earth**, the storyteller may have whispered as we crept into the field, **...than are dreamt of in our philosophy**. Not realizing it then, the irony of that seems clear now.

As Morris Jessup discovered, anonymous letters are as important to ufologists as photographs of flying saucers. There's much to be gained from receiving them, particularly if they contain crucial information, and mysterious letter writer Carlos Miguel Allende chose his target well – Jessup was a well-known author and lecturer on the subject of UFOs. But the tale of the vanishing ship – destroyer DE-173, the USS Eldridge, still provokes more questions than answers. It is simply packed with the inexplicable: spontaneous human combustion, visits by men in black, a mysterious suicide, secret logs and witness testimonies, classified reports that are always just beyond the reach of independent investigators... and, of course, the government. More than enough to satisfy everyone. But the story is worth considering from a slightly different point of view –

one that reveals the far too frequent deception and false reflections of some of *those* who investigate the paranormal.

The years immediately following World War II were the perfect time to promote the story of invisibility. Einstein's Theory of Relativity had helped to change our world forever, with consequences that even Einstein hadn't imagined. In theory, his later ideas of Unified Fields were even more revolutionary. And, as Allende suggests, they were so revolutionary that they were hidden from the general public.

This was indeed a strange time in our history, anything was believable and many things were possible. Wilhelm Reich was discovering the dangers of Deadly Orgone Radiation – research for which he was eventually jailed, and *that* laid the foundation for the Philadelphia Experiment's successor, the Montauk Project. The public were also becoming increasingly aware of the concept of other government 'black projects'; with millions of tax dollars vanishing into thin air, just like the Eldridge, apparently.

So, Allende's letters not only encouraged people like Jessup, but included enough scientific detail – false or otherwise – to convince the hard-nosed Office of Naval Research (ONR) investigators to take him seriously. If they could *find* him. And Allende, for his part, promoted the image of himself as a kind of fugitive. According to Jessup, when they visited RD#1, Box 223, New Kensington, Pennsylvania, the address he gave on his letters, investigators found the farmhouse abandoned. It should be reported, however, that Carl Meredith Allen's family still own the property. As Jacques Vallée noted in a recent report of the case, published in the *Journal of Scientific Exploration*: **The 'investigators' who claimed to have gone there may simply have been indulging in a little lie of their own.** Whatever startling information the Allende correspondence provided Jessup with, or actual secrets of military science, he has found his place in folklore history.

It was author and researcher Bill Moore who actually produced the news cutting which described the Philadelphia tavern brawl and disappearing sailors: **They just sort of vanished into thin air... right there**, reported one of the frightened hostesses, **and I ain't been drinking either!** which made his account of the mystery, *The Philadelphia Experiment* (with Charles Berlitz, 1979), all the more dramatic. As a point of interest, a decade later Moore was fortunate enough to be the first citizen to see the notorious MJ-12 documents, after developing film that had been delivered anonymously.

The fact that one of the crewmen of the Eldridge who 'disappeared' from the bar has since been interviewed need not spoil a good story. While his testimony is not as exciting as Allende's, it does help to explain why the Navy was anxious to keep the true nature of their work secret. Edward Dudgeon served on the Eldridge's sister ship, the USS Engstrom. In 1943, both were being re-fitted in an attempt to combat Germany's destructive U-Boats. These devices included high-pitched torque screws, making it harder for submarines to identify depth-charge weapons. What seems to be behind Allende's story is the procedure known as de-guassing, where the hull would be wrapped with high-voltage cables to scramble its magnetic signature. The ship would not be invisible to radar, which the Germans didn't have, but invisible to magnetic torpedoes. Dudgeon explained his disappearance from the tavern just as easily. In order to join the Navy a year earlier, he'd forged his birth certificate to hide his age. He vanished so quickly when fighting started because he was too young to drink.

Some might still believe, of course, that all this could be yet more disinformation – that he *would* say that, wouldn't he? It would be unwise to underestimate the ONR's role in this regard.

Reports about the Philadelphia Experiment and the Montauk Project have survived the onslaught of fact for long enough to qualify them as myth. But then what are myths without a touch of exaggeration?

CLASSIFIED

You can't hide the truth forever

Reader, your
brief is to be alert
for the following
spine-tingling books.